How to know yourself better in 10 steps

LAURENCE SMITS

Translated by LAURENCE SMITS

Introduction

If you do not put yourself in words, it gets transformed into problems.

Life is a great challenge.
Living your life is the same as well, if not more.
Developing oneself can be quite uncomfortable. But it is necessary, above all in a world of deep and constant evolution.
It is necessary to have the courage to know yourself better to change your style of life, to choose your direction.

The main mission of everybody is to reinvent her or his life.
How do we do that to make it possible?
First of all, you need to develop courage to give birth to your talents that you have been hiding for so long.
You must have the courage to develop your potential, live your passions, listen to your dreams, and live from your dreams.
It is possible if you may hear it!
In life, we must make choices, assume them, and learn from them in order to move forward better.
It is also important to make peace with your past. It is the best way not to spoil the present moment or dread the future.

To meet the challenges ahead of you, you must focus on your strengths. The world changes. It changes very quickly. You too can and must change.
It starts with knowing you better.

Welcome on the path to your well-being in 10 steps. At the end of these 10 steps, you will see the wonderful in you.
I welcome you to the path of re-enchantment.

> "Never forget that you have all the dreams in the world inside you" (*Fernando Pessoa*)

Who am I?

I have been a French teacher of English for more than three decades. Over all these years in the teenage education world, I have improved my leadership skills and my knowledge of psychology.
I have also trained in these different fields in recent years.

Since 2018, I have taken on a major challenge for me: running a blog on writing, called **LA PLUME DE LAURENCE, www.laurencesmits.com.**
After taking on this challenge, I set up a remote writing workshop on my blog in 2019.
In 2020, I wrote a book to help all those who want to write but do not dare for different reasons: **299 TIPS TO WRITE BETTER** (unfortunately, only available in French for the moment).

Why this e-book to know yourself better?

We are all in a movement where we want to change, to evolve. It can take different forms: in our personal, professional, physical, or mental life.

My practice of yoga and meditation for 25 years has led me to reflect on the human being as a whole and to an obvious conclusion: to evolve, we must know ourselves better.

You can achieve this by reading tons of psychology books.

You can also practice the 10 exercises I am suggesting in this e-book, in order to develop your uniqueness and understand why you are where you are today in your life.

Step 1: my own shield

The shield or coat of arms is an ancient emblem of a noble family or a knight in the Middle-Ages. It is a description identifying its owner, like a banner.
The shield is a sign of recognition of an individual.

As you are unique, you will create your own shield by following the different steps.
Like all the exercises I offer, just take your time.
Life is not a stopwatch for every action; take some time for reflection and do your shield conscientiously.

The material needed:
- *A drawing page A4*
- *Coloured pencils or fountainpens*
- *A pencil*
- *A pen*

- **1st step: reproduce the model of the shield below**

Divide the page into 4 equal parts with a place above to write your motto.
Insert 50% of words and 50% of drawings. *(It is very important de let your creativity run free).*

My motto (or inspiring sentence)	
My present job My city	3 qualities of mine
What I want to be. Or what I want to become. Or another job I want to do. Or the life I want to have.	My superpower (What qualifies me most)

Here is my shield (done in August 2020):

- **2nd step: explain in 3 lines maximum what you have felt making your own shield.**

- **3rd step: what do you think of your shield when you observe it?**

Write your impressions without thinking and especially without any judgment!

> **Conclusion of this exercise:**
>
> Get to know yourself to understand who you really are. Everyone has their free will to progress ...or not. Do not let the others ruin your life any more! Decide to start living it now!

Step 2: what I like/ what I do not like

Since we were kids, we have been operating on the pattern: I like/I do not like.
For everything. Not just for the food, the colours, or the clothes.
We all spend a lot of time saying, "I like this, I don't like that". Life is not just about this binary opposition. So let us think about it more deeply.

- **1st step: relax for a moment and complete the following grids in total honesty with yourself while taking your time.**

What I have liked in my life until now 1) 2) 3) 4) 5)	**Why?**
What I have not liked in my life until now 1) 2) 3) 4) 5)	**Why?**

- **2nd step: select one of the items in each section that has had an influence in your life and explain the reasons in 5 lines maximum.**

Conclusion of this exercise:

Judgment and rehashing are toxic elements in your life. You cannot spend your life hating your past. You have inevitably accomplished great things in your life: know how to recognize them and learn from less good episodes.

Step 3: what I have already accomplished

Without really admitting it, you have already accomplished remarkable things in your life.

You must have undoubtedly been successful. Your successes make you move forward.

We all tend to focus on the negative aspects of our lives. A bit like all this negative and toxic information that we are showered with on the television news. Ignoring your strengths can be harmful to you.

You hold the power to draw the positive out of every action of your life. It is an undeniable force to move forward from day to day.
It is good for our mind, and in turn, for our physique.

- **1st step: list 10 action verbs to qualify what you have already achieved in your life, to qualify 10 successes:** *(raising children, cooking, learning a foreign language, studying, living in the region of your dreams, etc. are successes).*

1)
2)
3)
4)
5)

6)
7)
8)
9)
10)

- **2nd step: choose a verb that marks you more than the others. Explain why in 3 lines.**

You can perfectly continue this exercise and list 50 of your achievements.
It seems difficult at the beginning. If you let your mind relax, you will see how many wonderful things you have achieved.

And it is not over!

> **Conclusion of this exercise:**
>
> We all have the capacity within us to capitalize on our strengths, talents, and skills. It is high time to make your dreams come true. By keeping tracks of your successes, you will strengthen your self-esteem. Forget your weaknesses and build on your strengths instead!

Step 4: I characterize my character and my personality

Who am I? This is the question we ask ourselves. It is difficult to really define oneself. Others do it better for us!
We spend our life getting to know ourselves!

Overall, we still judge ourselves too harshly.
This leads to an unfortunate feeling of unhappiness. Our vision of ourselves plays a fundamental role in our ability to love and fulfil ourselves.

- **1st step: choose from the 2 opposite adjectives the one that suits you best and tick the corresponding box.** *(Choose the character trait that suits you today)*

Expansive (turned towards others)	Introvert (more withdrawn)
Conscientious	Dizzy
Idealistic	Realistic
Rebel	Docile
Dynamic	Nonchalant, relaxed
Original	Conformist
Enthusiastic	Indifferent
Helpful	individual
Curious	Jaded, bored
Impulsive	Rational
Methodical	Muddled
Persevering	Quickly discouraged

Tolerant	intolerant
Authoritarian	Submissive
Dynamic	Passive
Attentive	Dreamy
Attracted to responsibilities	Not attracted to responsibilities
Daring	Shy
Quiet	Restless
Quick-tempered	Calm, even-tempered
Sociable	solitary
Hard-working	Rather lazy
Quick	Slow
Ambitious	Modest
Self-confident	No confident
Confident in others	Suspicious of others
Patient	Impatient
Reckless	Careful

According to your choices, do not judge yourself. Neither qualifying adjective is preferable to another. All the character traits are interesting. The important thing is to identify yours and write them down.

Even if some character traits may sound like flaws, it is always possible to improve yourself and change!

- **I define my personality in 4 questions**

The **MBTI (Myers Briggs type indicator)** is the most widely used psychological test in the world. It allows you to rank among 16 personalities and can help you orientate yourself or improve your relationships with others.
The American **Isabelle Briggs-Myers** developed this test based on the work of renowned psychiatrist **Carl Gustav Yung**.

This test is both very serious and very simple. You just need to identify what is most spontaneous for you in the following 4 "mental processes":

1. **Where do you get your energy from:** in your inner universe (introversion "I"), or from the outside environment (extraversion "E")?

2. **How do you collect information**: through your 5 senses (the "S" sensation), or by trusting your "6th sense" (intuition "N")?

3. **What drives your decision**: logical reasoning (thought or "T", or your values (feeling of "F")?

4. **How do you get launched into action**: by making plans (judgment "J"), or adapting yourself to circumstances (perception "P")?

Your answers can be summed up in **4** letters which, put together, constitute your **MBTI**:

- INFP
- ESTJ
- INTJ, etc.

There are 16 possible combinations and each one corresponds to a personality type.

Here is the correspondence of the profiles:

- INTP: the researcher
- INTJ: the organizer
- ENTJ: the entrepreneur
- ENTP: the inventor
- INFP: the idealist
- ENFP: the psychologist
- INFJ: the advisor
- ENFJ: the facilitator
- ISTP: the craftsman
- ISTJ: the administrator
- ESTP: the promoter
- ESTJ: the manager
- ISFP: the artist
- ISFJ: the protector
- ESFP: the actor
- ESFJ: the bon vivant type

The test results can, in part, help you find your way. Your MBTI type will help you identify several important traits of your own character.

Obviously, the MBTI test cannot be enough to choose your professional path, for example. But this test can help you improve your relationships with others and balance your personality. It is a personal development tool.

Conclusion to this exercise:

It is good to rest on oneself to understand who we are. By understanding who we are deep inside, we can then choose our life options. Finding the right way to define our personality is a challenge that will help us understand others better. By doing this, we can discover how to make the most of ourselves and how to mature more.

Step 5: I define my talents

Your skills are your gifts, your talents, and your abilities.

There are many forms of intelligence, and each of us has several. Burt, each develops only 3 or 4, in general. At school, only 2! For a long time, intelligence was viewed as a unique mental ability, much like a central computer that would drive all our actions.
However, everything happens in reality as if we did not have one, but several internal computers that intervene successively in various situations in our life.

The American psychologist, **Howard Gardner**, identifies these "multiples intelligences" in 1983. Everyone therefore has 8 forms of intelligence at their disposal. But everyone tends to only develop 3 or 4.

Here is the list:

- *Verbal-linguistic intelligence*
- *Logical-mathematical intelligence*
- *Bodily-kinaesthetic intelligence*
- *Spatial intelligence*
- *Musical intelligence*
- *The intelligence of others or interpersonal*
- *The intelligence of self-awareness or intrapersonal*

- *Naturalistic intelligence*

- **1st step: write a sentence by completing the following 10 propositions:**

You just need to determine, in writing, the following points without relying on your past academic results. Let your mind go:

1. I am good at …
2. It is difficult for me to …
3. I like to …
4. I have difficulty in …
5. I can do …
6. I like to learn …
7. I like to learn (again) …
8. I dream of …
9. I remember …
10. I want to do, travel …

- You can continue this exercise by defining your own criteria.

- **2nd step: target the proposition to which you had difficulty answering.**
  Try to understand why.
  On the contrary, target the one on which you could have written many things.
  Try to understand why.

Conclusion to this exercise:

You can write down 3 big or small successes every day or every week in a notebook. This will get you used to seeing life on the positive side. You will notice, through the days, that you will find your 3 successes more and more quickly. You will format your brain in a positive mode.

Step 6: I define my values and my motivations

Once your character traits are more clearly defined and your abilities more clearly established, you can move on to the deeper motivations that drive you in life.

The American professor of social psychology, **Edgard Schein**, identified 8 major motivations that he called *"career anchors"*.

The motivations are different from person to person. Not everyone is motivated in the same way by sport, artistic creation, service to others or organization …

I strongly advise you to ask yourself, to take some time to think about this exercise.

- **Step 1: I define my values and my motivations**

Answer the following 8 questions being as honest as possible with yourself.

1. What is most important in life?
2. What motivates you in life?
3. What are you looking for?
4. What do you expect from your job? Or your training? Or your studies?
5. What do you expect from your social life?

6. Do you have a dream? If yes, which one? If not, why?
7. Do you have any goals in life?
8. What is your main area of interest?

- **Step 2: identify your main motivation (or your 2 main ones). Are these chosen motivations part of your life right now? Are they goals to be reached or just dreams?**

Conclusion to this exercise:

No motivation is better or superior to others. If your main motivation is not part of your current life, there is plenty to ask yourself questions! It is time to bring clarity to yourself!

Step 7: I refine my personality

You may find it difficult to know who you are.
It is normal. The exercise is not easy.

Then keeping a journal might help. You could write in it how you feel every day, just for 15 minutes a day. Gradually you will become more aware of yourself. Studies have shown that people who keep a journal feel healthier physically and mentally.

It is also important to make lists to help you better understand who you are.

- **1st step: draw up lists following the instructions below:**

1. **What I like and do not like**: fold a sheet of paper in half. At the top of the first half, write "I like" and at the top of the second half "I dislike". It could turn out to be a rather large project, which is why you should limit yourself to just one category per list, e.g., movies, books, food, games, people, etc.

2. **What I would do if I were a billionaire:** you could even present it as a sketch or drawing. Just make a list of the things you would buy or the things you would do if money were not an issue.

3. **The things that scare me:** what are your deepest fears? Spiders, death, loneliness? Write them down.

4. **The things that make me happy:** make a list of the things that make you happiest. You can even describe specific situations in which you felt happy or in which you would feel happy.

- **2nd step: take time to think about the reasons you like and dislike certain things, or why some scare you, while others make you happy.**

By forcing yourself to answer WHY, you will come to understand yourself better and better define your personality!
Take a sheet of paper and divide it in half: on one side you write your interests and on the other side you describe your personality.
You will then realize whether the two are in phase or not.
If this is not the case, you will have to ask yourself the right questions to remedy this or call a coach for that!

- **3rd step: refine your personality**

Answer the following questions honestly with yourself. Take the time to answer.

- Who will you be in 5 years?
- What are your obstacles to moving forward in life?
- What are you afraid of?
- Are you happy in your job?
- Are you satisfied with your life in general?
- What is your state of mind right now?
- Do you want to change your life?
- What makes sense to you?
- Why are you doing what you are doing?
- Do you have confidence in yourself?
- Do you feel that you are making progress?
- Are you happy in your life?
- What would it take for you to feel better? At work? In your life?
- Do you feel able of evolving? To change your personality? To change your job?
- Do you inspire others?
- Do you feel able to bounce back?
- Do you complain? Why?
- Do you have any ideas or strategies to get better? To change jobs? To change your life?
- What would be your first action?
- Do you feel able f engaging in a training? In a coaching program?
- What meaning do you give to the word 'success'?
- What talents do you recognize for yourself?

- What are your obstacles in the area you want to improve?
- What is your view of the ideal of life?
- Do you feel free to make your own choices?
- Do you feel free at all?
- Do you recognize your mistakes?
- Are any of your behaviours harming you or others?
- Are you demanding too much of yourself? Towards others?
- Do you care about what others think of you to the point of feeling embarrassed?
- Do your attitudes end up to unpleasant reactions from others?
- Do you turn events around yourself?
- Are your reactions disproportionate to the events?
- Do you put up with loneliness?
- Can you stand not getting everything you want?
- Do you admit that people adopt values or beliefs that are different from you and see things differently from you?
- Do you tend to assert yourself against others?
- Do your ideals and what you need to do match up well together?

Conclusion to this exercise:

These are only a small sample of all the questions you can ask yourself. Each new question will help you reframe the beliefs that are blocking you or clouding your life. These questions, or this reframing, in writing, will help you become aware of the pros and cons of your thoughts and attitudes. It will also let you know what thoughts and behaviours to encourage or avoid.

Step 8: my tree of life

Each person has in her or in him invaluable resources, in particular the resource to develop projects which will make her or him stronger.

Building your tree of life will allow you to discover new territories of your identity, to ask yourself questions, to take stock once in your life, to give you the means to succeed and why not to change your destiny.
You will be able to rewrite the story of your life to feel inspired, to imagine new possibilities.
The metaphor f the tree will allow you to ring out your skills and resources.

I suggest to you 3 trees of life to fill in, taking your time in peace. Reproduce them and write in each location produced.

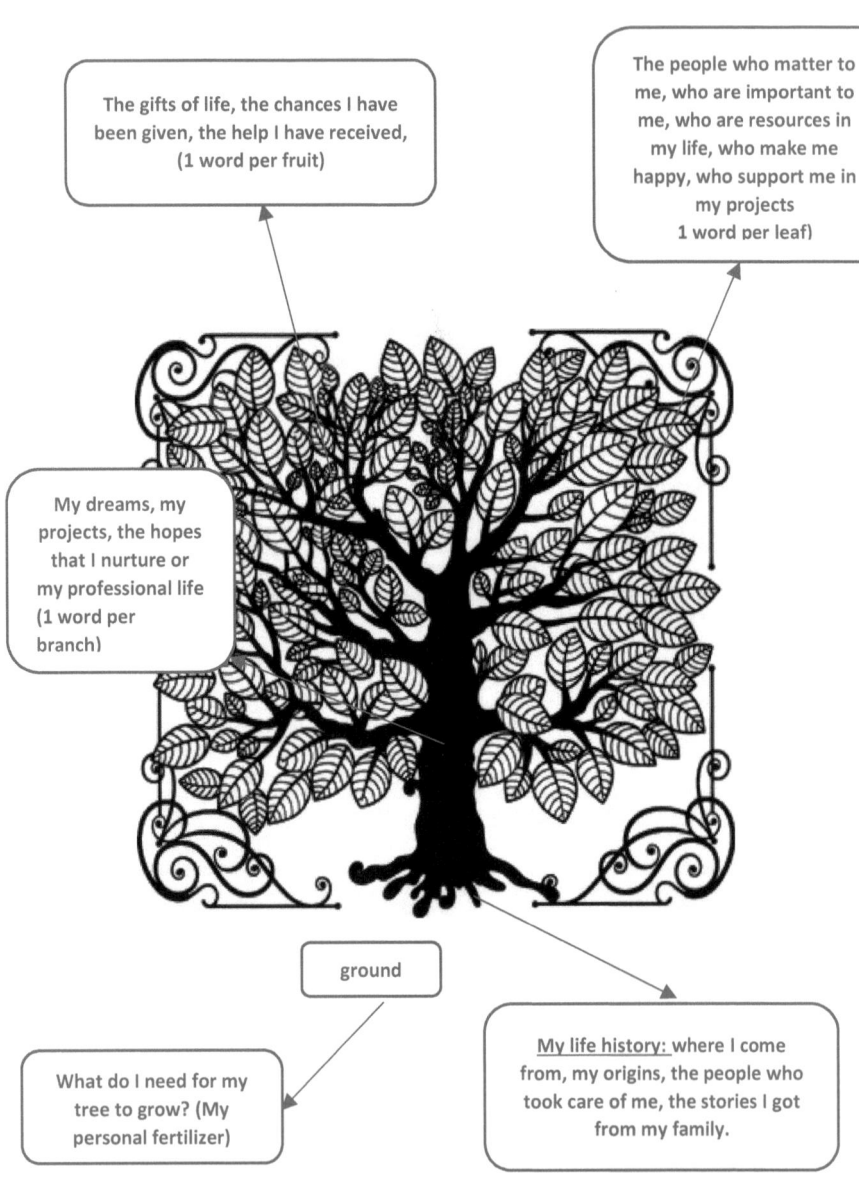

Conclusion to this exercise:

Filling your tree of life allows you to give meaning to your life, to your work, to redefine values that are a little buried under the routine of everyday life.
The tree of life allows to communicate better in your personal and professional life.
The tree of life represents a powerful symbol related to nature, to wisdom, to creation, to rebirth, to personal development, to strength, to beauty and to family.

Step 9: I discover my life mission

We all have a life mission.
But we do not know it and we do not realize it.
Your life mission is what you are on Earth for.

We have qualities, talents, strengths, successes.
The problem is that we tend to take too much into action, without sitting down a bit and taking the time to think.

Under the influence of others, family or society, even of social networks, people give up their dreams and desires, and are content with the daily routine that suffocates them. They end up forgetting their personality and are content to stay formatted.

Changing something in your life takes time. Nothing can be done overnight. Obstacles will be strewn on our way. Life is not a long quiet river, we all know that.
People, for the most part, fear to undertake, to accede to their dream or their project because of the gaze of others and of their own gaze!

- **1st step write down your top 10 talents according to you** *(a talent is an area in which you are good at and which gives you happiness).*

1)
2)
3)
4)
5)
6)
7)
8)
9)
10)

- **2nd step: ask your relations (family, co-workers) which talent defines you most.**

Writing your most ultimate talent is already bringing it to life, giving it a bit of reality.

- **3rd step: find out the common denominator among all the talents identified.**

This talent defining you is your life mission.
It can be helping the others, working in nature, being in contact with children, rescuing, feeling useful, protecting the environment, creating prototypes, cooking, etc.

Write down your life mission

MY LIFE MISSION IS

Conclusion to this exercise:

Finding your life mission will make you feel happier. Your happiness will radiate to you but will also flood those around you. You will release energies buried within you. Forget the gaze of others. Keep an open mind to all the possibilities for taking into action. You are the only one responsible for your life and your happiness!

Step 10: I put words on my obstacles and fears

To change tour life and make your dreams come true, you can no longer let your fears guide your life.
To move forward on your own path, you must know how to face your fears and overcome your limiting beliefs.
It starts by getting out, step by step, of your comfort zone, in which you are well settled.

We all have fears that are deep inside us and that come up whenever we want to take into action. They are our worst enemies.
Behind your doubts and indecisions hide your fears. They grow larger over the years and grow like weeds. We mistakenly think they protect us.

These fears make us hesitate, procrastinate in short, we do not change anything!
We are wrong not to wonder about the impact of our fears on our lives. Their power is phenomenal and insidious.

- **1st step: write down 5 limiting beliefs that keep you from moving forward in life**

*
*

*
*
*

2nd step: write down 5 limiting beliefs about yourself

*
*
*
*
*

- **3rd step: now rewrite these 10 limiting beliefs by turning them into positive sentences.**

For example: I do not know how to manage money, I cannot save = I am able to manage money; I can save a small amount of money every month.

Limiting beliefs	Positive beliefs

After this transformation exercise, you need to apply your new beliefs to strengthen them.
You underestimate the power of words and speech. When you have succeeded, step by step, in letting go one of your limiting beliefs, have a celebration. It is very important to celebrate every progress.

Remember that to change your life, you do not have to change everything.
The first key to change is yourself. You face your mind that you must absolutely recondition to see life differently.
It will take some effort. Big efforts. Certainly.
You have the solutions within you.
You are brave: you will achieve the goal you have set for yourself!

Your obstacles, your limiting beliefs and your fears are burdens. It is advisable to name them in order to defeat them. No obstacle is insurmountable.

- **4th step: list down 5 things you cannot do because of your fears and identify the fear behind it.**

Things I cannot do	Fears

What fears do we have?

The fear of failing, of succeeding, of illness, of being alone, of death, of poverty, of rejection, of changing jobs, of critics, of losing love, of the others' gaze, of growing old, to miss our life, etc.

How to overcome your fears?

You can hire a coach's services.
The other solution is to challenge yourself with achievable challenges in a limited time. Taking on one challenge after another breaks fears. You will gain self-confidence and develop self-esteem.

This is when the change can take place in your life. Keep in mind that all fears can be overcome. By overcoming one of your fears just once, you can make it go away.

Do not make the situation you find yourself in getting worse. Chances are that your life is not as bad as you think it is. Remember all your victories. None is small! Make peace with yourself. Calm down your mind. Let your fears be your allies. Go ahead with them at your side. They will not hurt you. Every evolution, every change comes along with fears. We build our own mental prisons!

We are lucky to be alive in countries where anything is possible.

Conclusion to this exercise:

This part about fears can touch. It can be disturbing. It is normal.
Changing just one of your habits takes at least 21 days. Fears have the capacity to cripple us. Getting rid of them is a real challenge. The biggest challenge is to be honest with yourself, to face the truth alone, without constantly judging yourself.
To change your life, you must stop fleeing away or taking refuge in your daily routine, where nothing changes. You will not make any good decision by hiding yourself behind your fears.
Becoming aware of your fears is already a big step that you have just taken!
Congratulations to you for having this courage!

Extra step: write a letter to yourself

If you want, you will write yourself a letter that you will not show to anyone.

You are going to write a letter to yourself to forgive your past, to forgive your mistakes, your misguided ways in life, in order to forgive the child that you were.

In this exercise, some emotions may rise to the surface.
You will learn to feel, to take a step back, to put down words, to clarify your thought, to take another look at yourself.
Even if emotions overwhelm you when you write, keep on writing.
You need to let the words come out of your mind and out of your body.
The words illustrate the evil that gnaws at you and that you must evacuate to go towards a better well-being.

LETTER TO MYSELF

The past belongs to the past. You can never change it. Do you think for just a moment that living with regrets or remorse makes you move forward in life?

Forgive people who have done wrong to you in the past, including your parents.
Accept your past as a life experience, a life learning experience.
Believe me, life is easier and lighter when you forgive. Forgiving is not at all a sign of weakness. It is rather a sign of great courage and great intelligence.

By forgiving yourself, you will stop feeling guilty about yourself.
Do not go on living like most people who live in the past!
You will then have taken a big step forward.

We can all change.
By thinking differently and positively.
By acting.
By believing in ourselves.
By believing in life.

Conclusion

I do hope that through these 10 steps you have come to know yourself a little more, or at least to have started a change.
It is all I wish for you, with all my heart.

I suggest 5 questions to conclude, which you will take the time to answer:

Take 20 minutes to answer each question, calmly.
Answer them honestly.
Take the time to think about the deeper meaning of each question.

1. **What thing do you dream of doing above all else?**
   - Why haven't you done it already?

2. **Why are you afraid of making mistakes?**
   - Don't you think that we learn by making mistakes?

3. **Have your greatest fears ever come true?**
   - Are they really your fears or those of the others around you or of society?

4. **Could you be your own friend?**
   - For what reasons, whatever the answer?

5. **Who will you be in 5 years?**
- Do you feel capable of projecting yourself into the future?

The most important thing in everyone's life is to have a radiant and fulfilled life, isn't it?
Accept reality, your current reality.
Keep confidence in yourself, you can make every part of your life evolve.
Look for strength within yourself.

The change will start with you.
Take the time to deepen your personality, in any way possible.
Take care of your mind.

Work your energy through the practice that is right to you. Keep enriching yourself.

Do not wait until you are ready to **DARE TO CHANGE**. We are never quite to do it!

I wish all the best in your life to come!

LAURENCE SMITS

My translation services in French and in English

My translation services English/French

- You do not master French enough to translate your professional or personal documents?
- You want to have your documents translated by a native speaker?
- You do not trust some online translators?
- You wish to develop your firm on a worldwide scale?
- You want to modify your leaflets and commercial brochures?
- You do not have a co-worker able to translate in a superior level?
- You want to increase the visibility of your firm in European French-speaking countries?
- You want to translate your e-books into French?
- You have problems to understand the administrative functions in France if you a foreign resident?

- **By using my translation services, you will quickly resolve your document translation problems.**

- **By using my translation services, you will have a faithful and serious translation of your documents, far from automatic translation such as Google Translate or Reverso.**

- Using the services of a professional translator is a simple and effective solution.
- By using my translation services, your work is given to a specialist.
- By using my translation services, you optimize your time and resources by letting me take charge of your translation project.

- Just contact me

Thanking

It is important for me to take the time to thank people who are dear to me.

Thank you to my companion **François** for his unfailing support. He gave me a wonderful office, a place where I can draw my inspiration from.

Thank you to my eldest son **Thibault** for his invaluable help in the Internet maze and his invaluable advice.

Thank you to my youngest son **Robin** for always supporting me morally.

Thank you to the **Spark program** that I followed in 2020-2021 and to its founder, **Franck Nicolas**, for having enlightened me so much and for having deeply transformed me.

Thanks to my **parents,** early supporters.
Thank you to my mother **Lucette** for making me love books.
Thank you to my father **Jacques** for showing me the way to tenacity.

Thank you to all my readers who follow me faithfully through my blog, **LA PLUME DE LAURENCE.**
They give me the strength to continue my writing work through their encouragement and loyalty.

Thank you to you dear readers of this book.
You bring me more than you think by trusting me.

Thank you to everyone who works behind the scenes to make this book exist.

To all of you, I wish you the best.

© 2021, Laurence Smits
Édition : BoD – Books on Demand, 12/14 rond-point des Champs-Élysées, 75008 Paris
Impression : BoD - Books on Demand, Norderstedt, Allemagne
ISBN: 9782322395798
Dépôt légal : Octobre 2021

Table of contents

How to know yourself better in 10 steps 1

Introduction 2

WHO AM I? 4

Step 1: my own shield 6

Step 2: what I like/ what I do not like 10

Step 3: what I have already accomplished 12

Step 4: I characterize my character and my personality 15

Step 5: I define my talents 20

Step 6: I define my values and my motivations 23

Step 7: I refine my personality 25

Step 8: my tree of life 30

Step 9: I discover my life mission 35

Step 10: I put words on my obstacles and fears 38

Extra step: write a letter to yourself 43

Conclusion 46

My translation services in French and in English 48

Thanking 50